Find
when a Loved One
Loses Faith

by
Rev Nick Donnelly

*All booklets are published thanks to the
generous support of the members of the
Catholic Truth Society*

CATHOLIC TRUTH SOCIETY
PUBLISHERS TO THE HOLY SEE

Contents

*Dedicated with much love to all members of my family
who have left the Church, to their children and grandchildren*

Scriptural quotations in this booklet are from the *Revised Standard Version*.

Image Credits: Pages 14, © Protasov AN/Shutterstock.com; Page 25, © Bart Sadowski/Shutterstock.com; Page 43, © Romolo Tavani/Shutterstock.com; Page 66, © Jurand/Shutterstock.com and Page 78 © Onchira Wongsiri/Shutterstock.com.

ISBN 978 1 78469 177 6

God knows we easily get lost

Every family I know is affected in some way by the modern loss of faith. I've lost count of the number of young people I've known who have left the Church. The practice of the faith has collapsed in my own extended family. My paternal and maternal grandparents were all devout Catholics who attended daily Mass. They had between them eight children, who all practised the faith, one of them becoming a nun. In the next generation there were twenty-two children, including myself. Of this generation, only seven are practising Catholics, three are members of other Christian ecclesial communities, such as the Church of England and the Baptists, while the remaining twelve are now secular. Most of my grandparents' great-grandchildren have not been baptised and have no contact with the Catholic Church.

The collapse of the faith in my family is the experience of most Catholic families today. There are approximately five million Catholics in England and Wales, with less than one million regularly attending Mass. While stark, these statistics cannot convey the heartbreak and anguish suffered by grandparents, parents and siblings coping with loved ones walking away from the Church and rejecting what is most precious in life.

I've listened to mothers in tears asking what they had done wrong because every one of their children has left the Church. I've heard grandparents telling me of their desperation driving them to baptise their grandchildren in the bath because they were frightened about their salvation. I've listened to parents' deep hurt as they told me about their teenage children mocking them for being Catholics and believing the Catholic faith. I've seen devout widows at the Requiem Masses of their husbands surrounded by children and grandchildren who sat embarrassed throughout the Mass not knowing what to do or how to respond.

It seems that no family has been spared this pain. And it is totally understandable, and appropriate, that we feel this pain – this hurt, anxiety and grief on seeing those we love leave the Church. It is a tragedy. It is a tragedy involving the whole Church in the West.

A tragedy involving the whole Church

Pope St John Paul II warned that Europe was losing hope due to the promotion of a "vision of man apart from God and apart from Christ" that had led many people to falsely put man in the place of God. There is a general forgetfulness about God: "European culture gives the impression of 'silent apostasy' on the part of people who have all that they need and who live as if God does not exist" (Pope St John Paul II, *Ecclesia in Europa*, 9).

The word 'apostasy' comes from the Greek and means 'standing apart'. It refers to people losing faith and leaving the Church. The Church's canon law defines conscious and deliberate apostasy as "the total repudiation of the Christian faith" (*Canon* 751).

Only twelve years after Pope St John Paul's warning, Cardinal Sarah described how the situation had worsened, with an even more widespread acceptance of apostasy. He observed that Western societies "are organised and live as though God did not exist. Christians themselves, on many occasions, have settled down to a silent apostasy" (Robert Cardinal Sarah, *God or Nothing*).

Highlighting a phrase often used by Pope Benedict XVI, Cardinal Sarah concludes that Western societies are undergoing a "crisis of God":

Above all, Western culture has progressively organised itself as if God did not exist: many today have decided to do without God. As [Friedrich] Nietzsche affirms, for many in the West, God is dead. And we are the ones who killed him, we are his assassins and our churches are the crypts and tombs of God. A good number of the faithful do not go to them anymore to avoid smelling the putrefaction of God; but doing so, man does not know anymore either who he is or where he is going: there is a sort of return to paganism and idolatry; science, technology, money, power, freedom unbounded, pleasure without limit are our gods. (Interview with Cardinal Sarah, November 2015)

Of course the living God is not dead, but Cardinal Sarah is pointing out two hard truths: more and more people are living as if God does not exist and the scandals and lack of faith of some Catholics presents a "corrupt" version of 'god' to society that stops people encountering the true God.

Pope Benedict XVI also warned of the crisis of faith gripping the Church in Western societies:

As we know, in vast areas of the earth faith risks being extinguished, like a flame that is no longer fed. We are facing a profound crisis of faith, a loss of the religious sense that constitutes the greatest challenge to the Church today. (Address to participants in the plenary meeting of the Congregation for the Doctrine of the Faith, January 2012)

Pope Benedict writes of a "profound crisis of faith that has affected many people" (*Porta Fidei*, 2). He observes that there is a crisis of faith in Western societies because many people "lack experience of God's goodness" due to losing contact with the Church. And many lose contact with the Church because they do not experience in the Church "spiritual strength, the strength of faith in the living God" (Meeting with Catholic lay faithful, September 2011).

The cultural forces at work in society and the Church that are destructive of faith have an impact on all our families, on our children and on our own lives of faith. We are constantly bombarded through the media by anti-Christian ideas and images. The government, civil society and educational bodies promote a secular world view from which God has been excluded. We live our lives among family and friends, fellow students and work colleagues who "live as if God does not exist". The temptation to lose faith, abandon the Church and reject God is ever present, and feels at times relentless.

God knows we easily get lost

In these circumstances, hostile to faith, it is so easy to get lost, even in the most devout and loving Catholic family, even with the best upbringing in the faith. The problem is that human beings by nature, due to original sin, have a tendency to get lost and separate themselves from God. It's important to know this about ourselves so we avoid self-righteous feelings of superiority or smugness just because we remain practising Catholics. There, but for the grace of God, go I.

Even if we are baptised, and therefore free from original sin, we are left with a wounded nature that leaves us vulnerable to the attraction of sin. As St Paul puts it, "I do not understand my own actions. For I do not do what I want, but I do the very thing I hate" (*Rm* 7:15):

> Yet certain temporal consequences of sin remain in the baptised, such as suffering, illness, death, and such frailties inherent in life as weaknesses of character, and so on, as well as an inclination to sin that Tradition calls *concupiscence*, or metaphorically, "the tinder for sin" (*fomes peccati*). (*Catechism of the Catholic Church* [*CCC*], 1264)

The Old Testament understands sin as rebellion against God, as disloyalty to God and as betrayal of God. Israel had three words for sin, which, translated into

English, mean: failing to meet our responsibilities to God; leading a life that deviates from God's purpose for us; and rebelling against the Lord. Each one of our sins is an expression, to different degrees, of failing God, deviating from his purpose and rebelling against him.

The Old Testament conveys the seriousness of rebelling against God:

> Zion shall be redeemed by justice, and those in her who repent, by righteousness. But rebels and sinners shall be destroyed together, and those who forsake the Lord shall be consumed. (*Is* 1:28)

Rebellion against God is not viewed in the Old Testament as a lifestyle choice or an expression of personal freedom that has no consequences, but is described as a personal offence or insult against God. Rejection of God is seen as arising from hatred of the Lord that arouses his anger.

The devil has power over us

It's sobering to realise that we all have an inclination to rebellion, to disloyalty and to betrayal. Why does original sin leave us with this inclination to rebellion against God? The Catechism explains that as a consequence of original sin, and the wound of concupiscence, the devil has power over us:

> By our first parents' sin, the devil has acquired a
> certain domination over man, even though man
> remains free. Original sin entails "captivity under
> the power of him who thenceforth had the power
> of death, that is, the devil". Ignorance of the fact
> that man has a wounded nature inclined to evil
> gives rise to serious errors in the areas of education,
> politics, social action and morals. (*CCC*, 407)

Satan is the original rebel against God, who wants to
tempt us all to join him in his absurd rebellion against
God, his creator and our creator. Pope Francis writes,
"The devil is a being that opted not to accept the plan
of God. The masterpiece of the Lord is man; some
angels did not accept it and they rebelled. The Devil
is one of them" (Cardinal Bergoglio & Rabbi Abraham
Skorka, *On Heaven and Earth*, p. 8).

The sacraments, particularly the sacraments of
Confession and the Most Holy Eucharist, protect us
from the power of the devil. But those who place
themselves outside the protection of the Church,
especially if they do so as a conscious act of rebellion
against God, put themselves under the influence of
the devil and in harm's way.

Though being a member of the Church gives us the
option of protection against the power of the devil,
it doesn't come automatically. There are Catholics

who appear outwardly to be members of the Church, but who secretly rebel against God by leading lives contrary to his commandments. And every time we commit a mortal sin we join Satan's self-destructive rebellion against God. Mortal sin destroys God's saving grace in our hearts, cutting us off from God and turning us away from our creator:

> When the will sets itself upon something that is of its nature incompatible with the charity that orients man toward his ultimate end, then the sin is mortal by its very object...whether it contradicts the love of God, such as blasphemy or perjury, or the love of neighbour, such as homicide or adultery. (St Thomas Aquinas)

The devil seeks to tempt us to commit mortal sin to destroy the life of grace within us, and thereby make us rebels against God with him. We need to be permanently on our guard against the temptations of the devil, who wants to "distance us from the path of Jesus":

> During his earthly life, he experienced temptation and persecution. We who want to follow Jesus, and who by our baptism have taken to the Lord's path, must be well aware of this truth: we too are tempted, we too are objects of the demon's attacks, for the

spirit of evil does not want us to become holy, it does not [want] us to bear witness to Christ, it does not want us to be disciples of Christ. (Pope Francis, Morning Meditation in the Chapel of the *Domus Sanctae Marthae*: 'The devil exists', 11th April 2014)

God comes looking for us when we get lost

The world in which we find ourselves, created by mankind's long history of sin, is often upsetting, even frightening at times, especially with our inclination to sin and the devil's constant temptation to rebel against God. But at the heart of the Good News that Our Lord proclaims is a marvellous fact – God comes looking for us when we get lost, when we rebel against him, and separate ourselves from his life and his love. The whole purpose of the Incarnation is God looking for lost, sinful humanity:

But God shows his love for us in that while we were yet sinners Christ died for us (*Rm* 5:8). God sent his only Son into the world, so that we might live through him (*1 Jn* 4:9). For God so loved the world that he gave his only Son, that whoever believes in him should not perish but have eternal life. For God sent the Son into the world, not to condemn the world, but that the world might be saved through him (*Jn* 3:16-17).

Since the early Church, Our Lord's Parable of the Lost Sheep has been understood as revealing the truth of the Incarnation from God's perspective. The parable (*Lk* 15:1-7) is one of the "parables of mercy", a series which also includes the parable of the lost coin (*Lk* 15:8-10) and that of the father and his prodigal son (*Lk* 15:11-32). Pope Benedict XVI comments that these parables of mercy constitute God's explanation of his own being as love and his activity towards sinful man (Pope Benedict XVI, *Deus Caritas Est*, 12).

Of these three parables, the Parable of the Lost Sheep best describes God's loving action towards us when we get ourselves lost:

> So he told them this parable: "What man of you, having a hundred sheep, if he has lost one of them, does not leave the ninety-nine in the wilderness, and go after the one which is lost, until he finds it? And when he has found it, he lays it on his shoulders, rejoicing. And when he comes home, he calls together his friends and his neighbours, saying to them, 'Rejoice with me, for I have found my sheep which was lost.' Just so, I tell you, there will be more joy in heaven over one sinner who repents than over ninety-nine righteous persons who need no repentance. (*Mt* 18:12-14; *Lk* 15:3-7)

Through the mystery of the Incarnation the Son of God assumes a human nature to come in search of humanity lost in sin, estranged from God, shut out of heaven. The Church Fathers interpreted the Parable of the Lost Sheep as describing God's decision to leave the glory of heaven in search of sinful humanity. Pope Benedict XVI writes:

> The human race – every one of us – is the sheep lost in the desert which no longer knows the way. The Son of God will not let this happen; he cannot abandon humanity in so wretched a condition. He leaps to his feet and abandons the glory of heaven, in order to go in search of the sheep and pursue it, all the way to the Cross. He takes it upon his shoulders and carries our humanity; he carries us all – he is the good shepherd who lays down his life for the sheep. (Mass, Imposition of the Pallium and Conferral of the Fisherman's Ring for the beginning of the Petrine Ministry of the Bishop of Rome, 24th April 2005)

According to Church tradition the ninety-nine sheep represent the angels in heaven who have no need of repentance, while the lost sheep represent wayward humanity. The angels rejoice in heaven when individuals respond to God's grace of repentance, reject their sinful lives and return home. In his commentary on the Gospel of Luke, St Ambrose writes:

> Rich then is that Shepherd of whose portion all we are but a hundredth part. For he has besides the innumerable flocks of the Archangels, of the Dominations, of the Powers, of the Thrones and all the rest whom he left upon the mountains. And since they are rational flocks, they not unfittingly rejoice because of the redemption of men. Let this also incite us to a just and upright life, that each one shall believe that his own conversion to God is pleasing to the angelic choirs, whose protection he should seek, and whose good will he should fear to lose. Be ye therefore a joy to the angels; let them have cause for rejoicing in your own return.

The Church Fathers did not interpret the ninety-nine sheep as practising Christians who remained members of the Church. They saw all of humanity as lost by nature – we are members of a lost race. But more than this, we are members of a race for which God descended from heaven through the Incarnation in search of us.

God has a special love for the lost

Christianity's most fundamental definition of the divine nature is "God is love" (*1 Jn* 4:8), and the Parable of the Lost Sheep shows us that God's love is dynamic, restless, in search of the lost. Pope St John Paul II explained that the reason why he never ceased to exhort "Do not be afraid" was because he knew that God is constantly searching for each lost sheep, that he leads the lost back to the sheepfold, looking after the weak and sick, bandaging their wounds, and protecting the strong. (Pope St John Paul II, Homily on the 25th Anniversary of His Pontificate, 16th October 2013)

Pope Francis likewise says that "Our God is a God who searches", that searching is a description of God's loving care towards man. Searching so defines God that Pope Francis proposes that God has a special love for those who get lost in sin:

God has a certain weakness of love for those who are furthest away, who are lost. He goes in search of them. And how does he search? He searches to the very end. Like the shepherd who journeys into the darkness looking for his lost sheep until he finds it or like the woman who, when she loses her coin, lights a lamp, sweeps the house and seeks diligently until she finds it. God seeks out the lost because he thinks: "I will not lose this son, he is mine! And I don't want to lose him!" (Morning Meditation in the Chapel of the *Domus Sanctae Marthae*, 7th November 2013)

Times when I've been lost

I was born a cradle Catholic and grew up in a loving, practising Catholic family that faithfully went to Mass on Sunday. I'm a husband, a permanent deacon, a catechist and a journalist. I was granted a mandatum by a bishop that officially acknowledges me as a teacher of theology within the full communion of the Catholic Church.

But despite all this, there have been times in my life when I was lost, and sometimes very lost. I still attended Mass, and to outward appearances I was a Catholic, but I was lost all the same. As a teenager I got involved in occultism, using Tarot cards, I Ching and occasionally Ouija boards. For several years I read the works of occultists and dabbled in occult practices. Looking back I can see that I was seeking direct spiritual experiences in the natural world. At the time I didn't realise that messing around with the occult put me in danger from the devil.

Growing up in a Church coming to terms with Vatican II my initial catechesis was poor, and at that time I had no knowledge of Catholic spiritual traditions. My love of the Blessed Sacrament and my experience of Our Lord's Real Presence kept me anchored in the Church, but it shames me to say now that this was not enough for me. I wanted more.

I attempted to integrate my New Age interests with my Catholic faith through Fr John Main's Christian Meditation, which offered me the spiritual disciplines and experiences I craved. Many Christians have deepened their relationship with Christ through Christian Meditation. However, through practising meditation, instead of coming closer to Christ I was attracted to Buddhism and Hinduism. I began to read their religious texts and attempted to practise mindfulness meditation. I corresponded with the Benedictine monk Dom Bede Griffiths (1906–1993) at his ashram in India, who encouraged my explorations of Eastern religions.

Eventually I came to the point where I was faced with the choice of remaining a Catholic or renouncing the Catholic faith by becoming a Buddhist. During a retreat at the Cistercian monastery on Caldey Island, South Wales, I discussed my situation with one of the brothers. In a few simple words the monk cut through my confusion. He asked me, "Why would you choose a religion that at its heart only offers an encounter with 'nothing', when Christianity offers you an encounter with the divine love of a person, Our Lord Jesus Christ?" From that moment I lost all interest in Buddhism – but I still had a spiritual restlessness.

The turning point in my life occurred, through the providential care of God, when I undertook the Spiritual Exercises of St Ignatius Loyola. St Ignatius, under the influence of the Holy Spirit, designed a sequence of imaginative meditations based on Sacred Scripture, prayers and rules for discernment rooted in Christian tradition. The goal of the Spiritual Exercises is to lead you to immerse yourself in the life of Christ and the promptings of God's grace to the point of being able to freely choose to serve the Lord in whatever way he calls you. Undertaking the Spiritual Exercises had a profound and lasting influence on my life, giving me an unquenchable desire to know Jesus more clearly, and follow him more nearly.

Looking back on my life, I can see that during the times that I got lost, Jesus came searching for me. Through his grace, and other Catholics, he called me back to himself. Having been lost I know the truth of these words from the *Catechism of the Catholic Church* (*CCC*, 30):

> Although man can forget God or reject him, He never ceases to call every man to seek him, so as to find life and happiness. But this search for God demands of man every effort of intellect, a sound will, "an upright heart", as well as the witness of others who teach him to seek God: "You arouse us so that praising you may bring us joy, because you have made us and drawn us to yourself, and our heart is restless until it rests in you". (St Augustine, *Confessions*)

God knows we easily get lost: Prayer reflections

Jesus, help me to feel your loving forgiveness as you come searching for me, for I am so often lost.

Jesus, help me to be a true member of your Church, seeking to embrace the fullness of your truth and beauty.

In spite of my weakness and failings, may I become a witness, teaching others the way to find you.

What does it mean to be Catholic?

Nowadays people use the word "Catholic" in many different ways. Some people say they are Catholic because their grandparents were faithful and went to Mass. Others call themselves Catholic because they went to a Catholic school during childhood, even if they haven't had any contact with the Church since. There are those who call themselves Catholic because they were baptised as babies and they attend family christenings, weddings and funerals. There are also people who call themselves Catholic because they occasionally attend Mass at Christmas.

Faced with this complex modern reality, the question arises, what makes a person Catholic? To answer this question, we should begin with the Catholic Church's understanding of herself. The Catholic Church's understanding is that all of humanity is in a relationship with her, because she is the sacrament, the visible expression, of Jesus Christ in the world. And Jesus is the expression of God's desire and will to search for lost humanity and bring everyone back into the safety of his divine purpose and grace.

There are two divine mysteries that explain why all of humanity is in a relationship with the Catholic Church.

Through the Incarnation, the Son of God assumed a human nature through his mother Mary. It is through that human nature that Our Lord Jesus Christ is mysteriously linked to every human being:

> For by his Incarnation the Son of God has united himself in some fashion with every man. He worked with human hands, he thought with a human mind, acted by human choice and loved with a human heart. Born of the Virgin Mary, he has truly been made one of us, like us in all things except sin. (*Gaudium et Spes*, 22)

Due to God's desire that everyone be saved, all people without exception are called to participate in the Catholic Church. Therefore, all people either belong to the Catholic Church or are related to her in various ways:

> All men are called to be part of this catholic unity of the people of God which in promoting universal peace presages it. And there belong to or are

related to it in various ways, the Catholic faithful, all who believe in Christ, and indeed the whole of mankind, for all men are called by the grace of God to salvation. (*Lumen Gentium*, 13)

This means that all people are, to varying degrees, related to the Catholic Church either through direct participation or connection with some aspect of divine revelation or Catholic world view, beliefs or morality. The happy truth is that the salvation of Christ is near to every human being.

The Church is necessary for salvation

To be clear, this does not mean that everyone who is related to the Church fully belongs to the Catholic Church. Nor does it dispense with the requirement established by Our Lord Jesus Christ, that baptism is necessary for salvation. It is impossible to belong fully to the Church without baptism. It is another ancient principle of the Church's self-understanding that there is no salvation outside the Church. The Church is necessary for salvation:

Basing itself upon Sacred Scripture and Tradition, it teaches that the Church, now sojourning on earth as an exile, is necessary for salvation. Christ, present to us in his Body, which is the Church, is the one Mediator and the unique way of salvation.

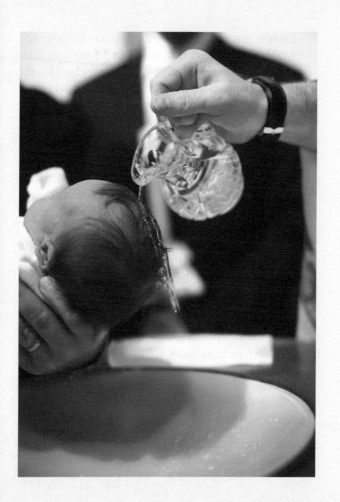

In explicit terms he himself affirmed the necessity of faith and baptism (*Mk* 16:16; *Jn* 3:5) and thereby affirmed also the necessity of the Church, for through baptism as through a door men enter the Church. Whosoever, therefore, knowing that the Catholic Church was made necessary by Christ, would refuse to enter or to remain in it, could not be saved. (*Lumen Gentium*, 14)

However, though the Church is necessary for salvation, it is possible for those who do not fully belong to the Church to hope in salvation because they are mysteriously joined to Christ and his Church through the Incarnation and through God's desire to save everyone: "God has bound salvation to the sacrament of Baptism, but he himself is not bound by his sacraments" (*CCC*, 1257):

Those who, through no fault of their own, do not know the Gospel of Christ or his Church, but who nevertheless seek God with a sincere heart, and, moved by grace, try in their actions to do his will as they know it through the dictates of their conscience – those too may achieve eternal salvation. (*Lumen Gentium*, 16)

It is important to realise that it is only those who freely, deliberately and with full knowledge reject Our Lord

Jesus Christ and his Church who cannot be saved. Our Lord does not force those who choose to be lost to be found by him, but he does persevere in searching for them and he will persist in inviting them to return home up to the moment of death.

Who fully belongs to the Catholic Church?

The Second Vatican Council spent some time clarifying what was necessary for people to fully belong to the Church. The Council Fathers concluded that people must share in the invisible and visible communion of the Church if they are to fully belong: the invisible communion of faith, hope and love and the visible communion of professing the faith, celebrating the sacraments and recognising the authority of the Pope and bishops:

> They are fully incorporated in the society of the Church who, possessing the Spirit of Christ accept her entire system and all the means of salvation given to her, and are united with her as part of her visible bodily structure and through her with Christ, who rules her through the Supreme Pontiff and the bishops. The bonds which bind men to the Church in a visible way are profession of faith, the sacraments, and ecclesiastical government and communion. He is not saved, however, who, though part of the body of the Church, does not persevere

in charity. He remains indeed in the bosom of the Church, but, as it were, only in a "bodily" manner and not "in his heart". All the Church's children should remember that their exalted status is to be attributed not to their own merits but to the special grace of Christ. If they fail moreover to respond to that grace in thought, word and deed, not only shall they not be saved but they will be the more severely judged. (*Lumen Gentium*, 14)

What Catholics think and feel

We belong to the Church through an invisible communion we share with all Catholics "possessing the Spirit of Christ" through the sacrament of Baptism. We can only fully belong to the Church through this special grace of Christ, which we cherish and nurture by living Christian lives of faith, hope and love. Simply put, the closer we are to Christ, the more we live and love as Christ, the more fully we belong to the Church.

Lumen Gentium warns of the danger of not responding to this special grace of Christ in thought, word and deed. This warning applies not only to those who leave the Church, but also to those who remain practising Catholics. In fact, *Lumen Gentium* singles out those who remain in the Church, warning that being a member of the Church out of habit is not enough. If faith, hope and love die in our hearts, then membership of the Church can only be an external, meaningless bond. Sadly I've met Catholics who are full of rage, resentment, jealousy and disobedience. Somewhere in their lives they have gone down the wrong path and have lost touch with the spirit of Christ and have forgotten how to love. Above all else, Christians are called to love as Christ loves – loving God and our neighbour with all their mind and strength, and having a special love for our enemies:

> If I speak in the tongues of men and of angels, but have not love, I am a noisy gong or a clanging cymbal. And if I have prophetic powers, and understand all mysteries and all knowledge, and if I have all faith, so as to remove mountains, but have not love, I am nothing. If I give away all I have, and if I deliver my body to be burned, but have not love, I gain nothing. (*1 Co* 13:1-3)

If we fail to love as Christ loves, then not only will we not be saved, but we will be more severely judged.

What Catholics do

We also belong to the Church through an equally essential visible communion of professing the faith, celebrating the sacraments and obeying the authority of the Pope and bishops when they uphold the perennial teaching of the Church. It is only through living by the fullness of faith, the splendour of the liturgy and the moral way of life of the Church willed by Christ that we can have the sure and certain knowledge of being fully in union with Jesus Christ, and belonging to his Catholic Church. As Canon John Redford put it, "[B]eing a Catholic means accepting the whole of the means of salvation offered by Christ" (Canon John Redford, *What is Catholicism?*, p. 39).

Sadly, looking back at the times when I got myself lost in New Age practices and Buddhism, I can now recognise that I only partially belonged to the Church. Though I attended Mass every Sunday, I mixed with Catholics who rejected aspects of the Church's teaching and doubted, sometimes mocked, the authority of the Pope and faithful bishops. I worked in a Catholic charity among people who did not accept the Church's teaching on contraception and sexuality. And I was a student at a Catholic college where some lecturers questioned the Church's sexual morality and what it meant to be Catholic. Under the influence of Catholics who were lost, I got myself even more lost in sin.

But I can also see in retrospect that Our Lord came looking for me, that he searched me out and found me trapped in a tight tangle of unfaithful thoughts and disobedient behaviour. Through his grace, the intercession of Our Lady, saints such as St Ignatius of Loyola and the friendship of faithful Catholics, Our Lord untangled me from my sin and brought me back into the full communion of the Church.

What does it mean to be Catholic? Prayer reflections

Father, teach me to cherish and nurture the special grace of Christ I have been given, by living a life of faith, hope and love.

Teach me to love, embrace and accept the whole of the means of salvation offered by Christ.

Give me the wisdom to see when I am trapped in a tangle of unfaithful thoughts and disobedient behaviour and lead me back to full communion with your holy Catholic Church.

Reasons why people leave

People leave the Church for all kinds of reasons, some of which are more understandable than others, but at the end of the day leaving is always a serious mistake. St Paul warns Christians of the danger of making a "shipwreck of their faith" (*1 Tm* 1:18-19). For whatever reason a person leaves the Church, they are always harmed by losing the priceless gift of faith.

Some leave the Church deliberately after much thought and struggle, while many leave the Church almost by accident, carelessly losing the habit, as if they misplace their faith. C S Lewis, the author of the Narnia novels, got lost after the death of his mother, returning to Christianity later in life. Looking back on the reason why he left the practice of the faith, he wrote:

> And as a matter of fact, if you examined a hundred people who had lost their faith in Christianity, I wonder how many of them would turn out to have been reasoned out of it by honest argument?

Do not most people simply drift away? (*Mere Christianity*, p. 127)

The Catholic author Pierre Lefèvre gives an account of his loss of faith at the age of 18 during his mandatory military service that shows someone drifting away from the faith:

I was posted to Paris. For the first time in my life I was living with people of no belief. Of the thirty soldiers in our section I was the only one to go to Church on a Sunday. In that situation I began doubting. My comrades were basically sincere and friendly. And yet they had no thought for God or religion. So it was possible to get along without faith. And besides why should I alone be in the right and all the others in error? So I gradually became unbelieving in my heart. Within me there was darkness. (Pierre Lefèvre, *One Hundred Stories to Change Your Life*, p. 63)

Pierre Lefèvre found his way back to the faith through his beloved aunt, Teresa, of whom he says, "God gave me a light in my night". Her life of quiet Christian love for the very poorest convinced him of the truth of Christianity: "Mustn't a faith which is such a power for love be true? And that was how I found my way back to the faith."

Casually drifting away from the faith is just one of the reasons why Catholics lose faith and leave the Church. Here are seven other reasons.

Determined to doubt

Sometimes individuals who have been brought up as Catholics come to a point in their lives when they are determined to doubt the faith. In her care for souls the Church makes the clear distinction between those who suffer from involuntary doubt and those who choose to think and express doubt. The *Catechism of the Catholic Church* explains the difference between the two (*CCC*, 2088):

Involuntary doubt refers to "hesitation in believing, difficulty in overcoming objections connected with the faith, or also anxiety aroused by its obscurity". A person suffering from involuntary doubt is not culpable because their struggles with faith occur spontaneously due to events or an unwanted train of thought.

Voluntary doubt about the faith "disregards or refuses to hold as true what God has revealed and the Church proposes for belief". This is a sin against the faith because the person chooses to reject or dispute a truth of the faith revealed by God and taught by the Church. Obstinate doubt describes an attitude towards an issue or question about the faith that refuses to consider the truth due to a determination to uphold an erroneous position contrary to the truth. Obstinate doubt is gravely serious because it deliberately, resolutely and defiantly rejects "a truth which is to be believed with divine and Catholic faith" (*Canon* 750§1).

Those who are determined to doubt often say that they will only believe what they can see, hear and touch, dismissing the faith of their childhood as nonsense and fairy stories. They often claim that scientific knowledge is the only true knowledge. The scientific method of collecting data, creating a hypothesis and verifying it is clearly useful and has benefited mankind. But to claim science is the only valid knowledge is a way of thinking called positivism or scientism. Pope St John Paul II warned of the impoverishment caused by scientism:

> Scientism consigns all that has to do with the question of the meaning of life to the realm of the irrational or imaginary. This leads to the impoverishment of human thought, which no longer addresses the ultimate problems which the human being, as the *animal rationale*, has pondered constantly from the beginning of time. (*Fides et Ratio*, 88)

The problem with solely believing in science is that the scientific method only examines sense data, things that can be observed and measured. As we all know, the richness of life, what makes life meaningful, is more than observable, measurable sense data. Scientism ignores or dismisses all the ultimate questions of human existence, such as 'Why am I here?', 'What is the purpose of life?', 'Why is there suffering and evil?', 'Why is beauty, goodness and truth so important to me?'

Failure of faith

Faith fails if there is no real encounter with Our Lord Jesus Christ. Faced with the fact that hundreds of thousands of young people pass through our Catholic schools, Bishop O'Donoghue, Emeritus Bishop of Lancaster, expressed his dismay about the drastic decline in young Catholics attending Mass. He concluded from this that the majority of young people do not have a living relationship with Jesus.

Pope Benedict and Pope Francis insist on the necessity of each one of us "encountering" Christ. Pope Benedict describes this encounter with Christ as being absolutely essential to being truly Christian; everything depends on our having an intimate relationship with Jesus:

> We are only Christians if we encounter Christ. Of course, he does not show himself to us in this overwhelming, luminous way, as he did to Paul to make him the Apostle to all peoples. But we too

can encounter Christ in reading Sacred Scripture, in prayer, in the liturgical life of the Church. We can touch Christ's Heart and feel him touching ours. Only in this personal relationship with Christ, only in this encounter with the Risen One do we truly become Christians. (Pope Benedict XVI, General Audience, September 2008)

I have met Catholics who have told me that they've never "met Jesus", that they've never "experienced" the presence of Jesus in their lives. Pope Francis recommends that a change of perspective will make all the difference. If you change your perspective from hoping that you'll only meet Jesus in heaven, to assuming that you will meet Jesus every day, it will revolutionise your Christian life.

Bishop O'Donoghue concluded that the way to help young people to have a living relationship with Christ was for adults to really believe in the power of prayer and in the expectation that we will encounter Jesus.

Shocked by scandal

Some Catholics lose their faith and reject the Church because of the scandals caused by fellow Catholics. I know individuals who have left the Church because they have suffered sexual abuse by clergy or because they are the parents of children who have been sexually abused. Our Lord was very aware of the harm caused to innocent believers by the sins and crimes of others in the Church. He gave this warning:

> But anyone who is the downfall of one of these little ones who have faith in me would be better drowned in the depths of the sea with a great millstone round his neck. Alas for the world that there should be such causes of falling. Causes of falling there must be, but alas for anyone who provides them. (*Mt* 18:6-7)

When we look at the history of the Church, we are often faced with a dreadful scandal. William of Auvergne, Bishop of Paris, writing in the thirteenth century, said that the barbarism of the Church had to make everyone who saw it go rigid with horror: "We are no longer dealing with a bride but with a monster of terrible deformity and ferocity" (quoted by Cardinal Ratzinger in *Introduction to Christianity*).

In a meditation on the Stations of the Cross in 2005, Pope Benedict XVI referred to the sins of men "soiling" the Church:

> The soiled garments and face of your Church throw us into confusion. Yet it is we ourselves who have soiled them! It is we who betray you time and time again, after all our lofty words and grand gestures.

Have mercy on your Church; within her too, Adam continues to fall. When we fall, we drag you down to earth, and Satan laughs, for he hopes that you will not be able to rise from that fall; he hopes that being dragged down in the fall of your Church, you will remain prostrate and overpowered. But you will rise again. You stood up, you arose and you can also raise us up. Save and sanctify your Church. Save and sanctify us all. (Cardinal Ratzinger, Meditations and Prayers for Way of the Cross at the Colosseum, Good Friday 2005)

How can God entrust his Church to the "dirty hands" of some men who have perpetrated wicked crimes throughout history, especially the deadly cruelty of anti-Semitism and the appalling physical and psychological damage of child sexual abuse?

Pope Benedict XVI says we are faced with the painful paradox of the Church being both holy and sinful at the same time. Salvation history shows us that God does not reject sinful humanity or individual sinners, but allows his revelation, the pure and holy self-communication of his inner life and grace, to be held in weak, fragile vessels – human beings. In his mercy, he chooses to associate with habitual sinners. Our history is one of repeat offending!

It's important to remember that the holiness of the Church is not the holiness of individuals, but is the unmerited, divine gift of holiness in the midst of human unholiness. The Church is not called "holy" in the Creed because we are holy or sinless, but because God exerts his holiness in her in spite of human sinfulness.

Jesus has given this power of sanctification, this power to make holy, irrevocably to the Church. We don't deserve it, we've done nothing to merit it, but because he loves us so much God chooses again and again as the vessels of his holiness "the dirty hands of men". The holiness of Christ radiates from the midst of the Church's sin.

Enraged by evil

St Thomas Aquinas, one of the greatest thinkers of the Church, admitted that the strongest objection to the existence of God was the problem of evil. The modern philosopher Peter Kreeft observes: "More people have abandoned their faith because of the problem of evil than for any other reason. It is certainly the greatest test of faith, the greatest temptation to unbelief. And it's not just an intellectual objection. We feel it. We live it."

The deaths of my brother and sister, Paul and Catherine, and the deaths of my children, Gabriel and

Ariel, forced me to question the existence of God. Grief can cut us off from God. Just at the time when we need to feel the love and closeness of God, he can feel distant, even absent. Looking back on my own times of intense grief, I don't think God had chosen to be distant or absent; it was just that the grief over my babies was so intense that I couldn't feel his presence through all the "noise" of my emotions.

Just when we need the solace of prayer and the sacraments, we can find that going to Mass or trying to pray triggers grief, stirring up feelings of anger towards God – Why did he let my brother and sister die? Why did he let my babies die? Why couldn't he save them through a miracle? It can also stir up feelings of guilt – did I have enough faith? Did I do something wrong? Am I being punished? All these thoughts and feelings around an "evil" event in our lives can drive people away from the Church.

The Church understands the pain caused by the bitter reality of evil, knowing the threat it poses to faith:

If God the Father almighty, the Creator of the ordered and good world, cares for all his creatures, why does evil exist? To this question, as pressing as it is unavoidable and as painful as it is mysterious, no quick answer will suffice. Only Christian faith as a whole constitutes the answer to this question:

the goodness of creation, the drama of sin and the patient love of God who comes to meet man by his covenants, the redemptive Incarnation of his Son, his gift of the Spirit, his gathering of the Church, the power of the sacraments and his call to a blessed life to which free creatures are invited to consent in advance, but from which, by a terrible mystery, they can also turn away in advance. *There is not a single aspect of the Christian message that is not in part an answer to the question of evil.* (*CCC*, 309)

The only answer I have found is the cross of Christ. There have been times when I couldn't find the words to pray because the pain was too great, but holding a crucifix tight in my hand helped. I can't explain why, because the mystery of the cross goes beyond words. The Catholic poet and playwright Paul Claudel gives a glimpse of the truth of the cross: "Jesus did not come to explain away suffering or remove it. He came to fill it with his presence." His closeness calms the storms of grief, his presence promises victory over death.

Seduced by secularism

Catholics are minorities in Western secular societies that constantly promote atheistic humanism through politics, the mainstream media and education. As Pope St John Paul II wrote, "European culture gives the impression of 'silent apostasy' on the part of people

who have all that they need and who live as if God does not exist" (*Ecclesia in Europa*, 9).

God has been eclipsed by man's focus on the material world. The materialist is so caught up in seeking enjoyment, in consumption, in the here and now that he or she gives no thought to the big questions of existence, such as the meaning of life, or what happens at death.

Christians in the rich West are not immune to the attractions of a society that focuses on the material needs and pleasures of man. Pope Benedict XVI warned that the invasion of atheistic secularism into every aspect of daily life had also invaded the Church through cultivating in many Catholics a "hedonistic and consumerist mindset" that affects the lifestyle and daily behaviour of believers (Address to participants in the plenary assembly of the Pontifical Council for Culture, March 2008). A consumerist mentality can also lead to approaching world religions as lifestyle choices that can be picked and mixed according to preference and taste. I'm sad to admit that I got caught up in this attitude before my true conversion.

Cardinal Henri de Lubac describes the delusion at the heart of atheistic humanism:

Man is getting rid of God in order to regain possession of the human greatness that, it seems to him, is being unwarrantably withheld by another. In God he is overthrowing an obstacle in order to gain his freedom. Modern humanism, then, is built upon resentment and begins with a choice. (*The Drama of Atheistic Humanism*)

Cardinal de Lubac observes that the humanist expectation that banning God results in greater freedom is a dangerous delusion. Our own society shows the dehumanising consequences of atheistic secularism – though celebrating more and more personal freedom, our society is marked by increasing bureaucratic organisation and regulation; though lauding rationality there is increasing absurdity; though expressing hope in the future there is an increasing sense that nothing really has meaning. Without God, man becomes increasingly inhuman, as expressed in the unquestioning acceptance of abortion, and the drift towards euthanasia.

It is only the Christian, with his hope beyond failure and death through the resurrected Christ, who can give true meaning and purpose to the world:

The truth is that only in the mystery of the incarnate Word does the mystery of man take on light. Such is the mystery of man, and it is a great one, as seen by believers in the light of Christian revelation. Through Christ and in Christ, the riddles of sorrow and death grow meaningful. Apart from his Gospel, they overwhelm us. Christ has risen, destroying death by his death; he has lavished life upon us so that, as sons in the Son, we can cry out in the Spirit; Abba, Father. (*Gaudium et Spes*, 22)

Downward descent

St Paul highlights an underlying cause behind many of the reasons why people get shipwrecked on the voyage back to God – moral misconduct leads people to find excuses to reject God and leave the Church: "By rejecting conscience, certain persons have made shipwreck of their faith" (*1 Tm* 1:18).

Blessed John Henry Newman wrote that conscience is "a law, an authoritative voice" bidding us to "do certain things and avoid others". Conscience commands, praises, blames, promises, threatens. "It is more than a man's own self. The man himself has no power over it, or only with extreme difficulty; he did not make it, he cannot destroy it" (*Sermons Preached on Various Occasions*).

For the Christian, baptised into the life of Christ, conscience attains its true purpose, because it "is a messenger of him, who, both in nature and in grace, speaks to us behind a veil, and teaches and rules us by his representatives. Conscience is the aboriginal Vicar of Christ" (Blessed John Henry Newman, *Letter to the Duke of Norfolk*; cf. *CCC*, 1778).

However, as we all well know, the fever of sin can deafen us to the voice of conscience:

> The reflection of sky and mountains in the lake is a proof that sky and mountains are around it, but the twilight, or the mist, or the sudden storm hurries away the beautiful image, which leaves behind it no memorial of what it was...Who can deny the existence of Conscience? Who does not feel the force of its injunctions? But how...easily can we be talked out of our clearest views of duty! How does this or that moral precept crumble into nothing when we rudely handle it! How does the fear of sin pass off from us, as quickly as the glow of modesty dies away from the countenance! And then we say, "It is all superstition." (Blessed John Henry Newman, *Christianity and Medial Science: An Address to the Students of Medicine*)

I knew someone who used to put pictures of Jesus and holy statues away in a cupboard when they wanted to do something wrong. They couldn't bear Jesus looking at them because it made them feel guilty. Many leave the Church because awareness of Our Lord makes them feel ashamed about their moral misbehaviour. But instead of the natural and right feelings of shame leading them to repentance and the rejection of sin, they reject God and his Church.

Unfortunately for our generation, the voice of conscience has been drowned out for many by the mistaken Freudian notion that shame is harmful. Thankfully Pope Francis does not view shame as a taboo, and often refers to the importance of accepting shame for conversion and receiving God's mercy. Shame and guilt can be good for us if they are signs of a healthy spiritual immune system fighting the destructive presence of sin in our lives. Shame can be particularly helpful because it keeps us humble before God and each other:

> Shame is a true Christian virtue, and even human... the ability to be ashamed. Don't be one of the "unashamed", because they are people who do not have the ability to be ashamed and to be ashamed is a virtue of the humble, of the man and the woman who are humble and childlike before God. (Morning Meditation in the Chapel of the *Domus Sanctae Marthae*, 29th April 2013)

Greater than God

Some individuals reject God due to what Fr Benedict Groeschel called the "Arrogance of Intellect". Intellectual pride can lead people to make the serious error of thinking they are superior to God and his revelation expressed in Christianity. It is common in this modern, scientific culture for people to dismiss God and Christianity as superstitious relics that should be consigned to humanity's primitive past.

But often, underlying this superior dismissal, there is a hatred of God, a bitter contempt towards Our Lord Jesus Christ. The *Catechism of the Catholic Church* explains:

> Hatred of God comes from pride. It is contrary to love of God, whose goodness it denies, and whom it presumes to curse as the one who forbids sins and inflicts punishments. (*CCC*, 2094)

It is surprising to find that those who intellectually dismiss Christianity as primitive superstition are not indifferent to God, but express strident hostility through ridicule and blasphemy. The impulse of humility and obedience towards God that creatures owe their creator and redeemer infuriates those who reject God. John Milton, the seventeenth century English poet, captures the desperation of this arrogant pride in his portrayal of Satan in *Paradise Lost*: "Better to reign in Hell than serve in Heaven." A modern version would be "I will not serve, I cannot see", which expresses the attitude of those Catholics who will not be obedient to God, so they refuse to genuinely engage with the evidence for his existence.

C S Lewis, a former atheist, was well acquainted with those whose intellectual pride leads them to hatred of God. In his novel *That Hideous Strength*, Lewis describes the suicide of Professor Frost, who has knowingly participated in a diabolical attack against mankind and God. At the moment of death he realises his mistake in arrogantly denying the supernatural and God, but instead of seizing the moment of realisation to repent and accept the loving mercy of God, Professor Frost could not let go of his hatred:

> He became able to know (and simultaneously refused the knowledge) that he had been wrong from the beginning, that souls and personal responsibility existed. He half saw; he wholly hated.

However, there is always the hope that up to the moment of death those who have rejected God, even hated him, can repent of their sins and accept God's mercy. It is important that we pray for the dead as an essential spiritual act of mercy, especially for those who lost faith, left the Church and rejected God. We must never let go of the hope that God comes in search of the lost out of his deep love for sinful humanity, with his offer of the grace of repentance and conversion.

Parable of the Prodigal Son

The Parable of the Prodigal Son (*Lk* 15:11-32), like the Parable of the Lost Sheep, shows that God comes searching for the lost. It gives us hope that no matter the reason for someone leaving the Church, no matter how adamant their rebellion, no matter how grave their sin, God longs for them to come home.

Pope Benedict XVI writes that in the Parable of the Prodigal Son we can see the "modern rebellion against God and God's law". Many who leave God and the Church and get on with their lives are like the Prodigal Son:

> He no longer wants to be subject to any commandment, any authority. He seeks radical freedom. He wants to live only for himself, free of any other claim. He enjoys life; he feels that he is completely autonomous. (Pope Benedict XVI, *Jesus of Nazareth: From the Baptism in the Jordan to the Transfiguration*, p. 204)

Our Lord's parable shows that when we seek total freedom to express the will of our egos and the desires of our flesh we will only find, at the end of the day, alienation and impoverishment. At the heart of the Parable of the Prodigal Son is the turning point of conversion that occurs with the realisation that the search for freedom from God is an illusion. These turning points come, these moments of realisation come, as graces from the God who searches constantly for those who are lost.

The important thing is not to doubt that Jesus is seeking the conversion of our loved ones who leave the Church. The fundamental imperative of Jesus's mission was to preach repentance, conversion and his personal forgiveness of sins. Jesus sought out the company of sinners, while at the same time denouncing sin wherever it might be masquerading as self-righteousness. In this way, Jesus is the physical embodiment of divine compassion and mercy, ultimately expressed through his death on the cross (*Jn* 1:29).

Reasons why people leave: Prayer reflections

Lord may I never leave you.

For those in my family who are in times of doubt, may they persist in the struggle to understand and accept you.

For those in my family who are suffering a failure of faith, may my belief in the power of prayer, and my expectation of encountering you, Jesus, help them.

For those in my family shocked by scandal, may they find it in their hearts to forgive.

For those in my family who are tested by the problem of evil, may they feel their suffering filled with your presence.

For those in my family who are seduced by the lure of secularism, may your Resurrection restore in them hope.

For those in my family who leave the Church to reject the voice of conscience, may they find repentance.

For those in my family who in pride dismiss you and Christianity as superstitious, may they learn humility and choose to accept your mercy.

You are God who comes searching for us when we are lost, may we be converted to love you and lose ourselves in your will.

Famous Christians
who got lost and came back

Pope Francis says the Church should be a "field hospital" set up in the middle of the raging battle of our lives. Like God who goes in search of the lost, when at her best, the Church goes out into the middle of the battlefield. Pope Francis said:

> I like to use the image of a field hospital to describe this "Church that goes forth". It exists where there is combat. It is not a solid structure with all the equipment where people go to receive treatment for both small and large infirmities. It is a mobile structure that offers first aid and immediate care, so that its soldiers do not die. (Pope Francis, *The Name of God is Mercy*)

Countless souls, suffering from the wounds of sin, desperately want care and healing and need to find a place of safety. A number of modern saints and famous

Christians left the Church, rejected God and became seriously lost, but at their lowest points they found the field hospital Church in the middle of their battle field. These include Blessed Charles de Foucauld, Blessed Bartolo Longo and Servant of God Dorothy Day.

Blessed Charles de Foucauld

Blessed Charles de Foucauld was a hermit witnessing to the faith among the Muslims in the Sahara desert. He was martyred by tribesmen in 1916. Blessed Charles regretted that he made no converts or companions during his life. However, his example of simple Christian witness at the peripheries of society inspired the foundation of two religious orders, the Little Brothers of Jesus in 1933 and the Little Sisters of Jesus in 1936. Both congregations have founded small communities throughout the world of two to four brethren who adore the Blessed Sacrament and share the daily life and work of ordinary people.

Charles de Foucauld was born into a very devout French Catholic family, and it is clear from his spiritual autobiography that as a young boy he deeply loved God, the Church and the Catholic faith:

And the true piety of my upbringing! The visits to churches, the flowers laid at the foot of the cross, the Christmas crib, the month of Mary, the little altar in my room that stayed there as long as I had a room of my own there, even outliving my faith; the catechisms, the first confessions guided by my Christian grandfather, the examples of true devotion given me by my family. I see myself going to church with my father, and with my grandfather. I see grandmother and my cousins going to Mass every day. And my first Holy Communion, after a long and careful preparation, surrounded by the blessings and encouragement of a family wholly Christian, in the presence of those I loved best in the world. (*Spiritual Autobiography of Charles de Foucauld*, pp. 10-11)

Following the deaths of his parents when he was 6 years old, Charles and his sister, Marie, were adopted by their maternal grandparents, who were also devout Catholics. At the age of 14, Charles went away to study at Nancy Lycée, in the agnostic atmosphere of which he began to lose his faith: "I remained twelve years without denying or believing anything, despairing of the truth and not even believing in God. There was no convincing proof."

He describes himself as first "drifting away" from God, and then withdrawing even further from God: "[M]y life began to be a death, or rather, had already become a death in your eyes [God]." By the age of 17, Charles admits he was "totally selfish, full of vanity and irreverence, engulfed by a desire for what is evil".

He continues, "I was completely disorientated. I was running wild. I was in the dark. I no longer saw either God or men: There was only me."

He graduated from the military academy of Saint-Cyr, the French equivalent of the UK's Sandhurst and the USA's West Point, but was a lacklustre officer. Charles led a dissolute life, interested only in taking pleasure in food, parties and the company of his mistress, Mimi. About this period of his life Charles wrote, "I sleep long. I eat a lot. I think little." He loved the good life so much he was known as "Fat Foucauld". Posted to Algeria, Charles caused scandal by taking his mistress with him, and when he refused to marry Mimi he was discharged from the army for "ignominious conduct".

Returning to France, Charles de Foucauld spent a couple of months of scandalous living, but finding society life boring he re-enlisted in the army. By the age of 25 Charles became a respected military leader, resigning from the army in 1882 to become a courageous explorer of Morocco with the French Geographical Society.

God who searches for the lost

Looking back on this period of his life, Charles de Foucauld admits that though he had no faith at all, he recognised that God was still at work in his life through various graces. Addressing himself to God he writes that despite his dissolute and immoral life, "you kept alive in me the taste for study, for serious reading and good things, and with it a disgust for vice and shame. I did evil, but I never approved of it or loved it." And, more than this, he can see his discontent and boredom as a grace from God calling him back:

> You made me experience a melancholic emptiness, a sadness that I never felt at other times. It would come back to me every evening when I was alone in my rooms; it kept me silent and depressed during our so-called celebrations: I would organise them, but when the time came, I went through them in silence, disgust and infinite boredom. You gave me the ill-defined unrest that marks an unquiet conscience which, though it may be wholly asleep, is not completely dead. I never felt that sadness, that distress, that restlessness apart from those times. It was undoubtedly a gift from you, O God! How far off I was in my doubting! How good you are! (*Spiritual Autobiography*, pp. 11-12)

After his adventures as an explorer Charles returned to Paris and settled close to his family, where he found the company of "people who were highly intelligent, highly virtuous and highly Christian". He admits in his spiritual autobiography that after six months of family life, he "admired virtue and longed for it". He still did not believe in God, but he felt an interior pressure urging him to return to God:

> And what interior graces: the need for solitude, recollection and pious reading; the urge I felt to go into your churches – I who did not believe in you; my unrest of soul, my anguish; my search for truth; my prayer: "O God, if you exist, let me know of your existence." All of these things were your work, O God – the work of you alone. (*Spiritual Autobiography*, p. 15)

Back with his family, and open to the culture of Christianity, even though he still did not believe in God, Charles de Foucauld took a major step by renouncing his past life of sexual immorality and by embracing chastity:

> My soul had to be made ready to receive the truth: the devil is too much the master of an unchaste soul to let truth enter it. You could not, O God, come into a soul where the devil of unbridled passions ruled supreme. But you wanted to come into my soul, O Good shepherd, and you yourself expelled your enemy from it. (*Spiritual Autobiography*, p. 13)

God had come in search of Charles and through his graces had led him to the point of a decisive encounter – his confession to the saintly Abbé Henri Huvelin, a priest at Saint-Augustin, Paris who spent long hours in the confessional and was much loved by ordinary Catholics. Abbé Henri Huvelin's pastoral approach is summed up in this saying of his, "If you meet someone who is searching, don't preach a sermon at him, just show him you love him." Charles gives this account of his encounter with Abbé Huvelin, addressing his thankfulness to God:

> The unparalleled blessing of directing me for my instruction in religion to Father Huvelin. I believe, O God, that by leading me to go into his confessional on one of the last days of that October you were giving me the best of all good things. If there is joy in heaven at the repentance of a sinner, then how great joy there must have been when I entered his confessional! What a blessed day that was – a day of blessing. And since that day my whole life has been a chain of blessings. I asked for instruction in religion: he made me get down on my knees and make my confession and sent me straight away to Holy Communion. When I think of it, I cannot stop myself from crying. (*Spiritual Autobiography*, p. 16)

From that moment Charles de Foucauld re-converted to the Catholic faith; as he explained, "The moment I realised that God existed, I knew I could not do otherwise than to live for him alone." Four years later he entered a Cistercian abbey and began his adventures as a monk.

Hound of Heaven

Blessed Charles de Foucauld's life shows us in dramatic form Our Lord Jesus Christ coming searching for the lost. The Good Shepherd can be gentle in his approach to souls, and he can also be relentless. The Catholic poet Francis Thompson captures the relentless and overpowering search of God in his poem, *Hound of Heaven*:

> I fled Him, down the nights and down the days;
>   I fled Him, down the arches of the years;
> I fled Him, down the labyrinthine ways
>   Of my own mind; and in the mist of tears
> I hid from Him, and under running laughter.
>   Up vistaed hopes I sped;
>   And shot, precipitated,
> Adown Titanic glooms of chasmèd fears,
>   From those strong Feet that followed,
>   followed after.
>   But with unhurrying chase,
>   And unperturbèd pace,
> Deliberate speed, majestic instancy,
>   They beat – and a Voice beat
>   More instant than the Feet –
> "All things betray thee, who betrayest Me."

This is the dynamic of the prodigal son that we can all identify with because all of us are sinners, and all of us are in need of deeper conversion. In my life, I can see God has given me moments of grace when I've been lost, interior realisations and exterior guides, which have helped me to choose to come back to my true home, having strayed into "alien lands".

Blessed Bartolo Longo

In the city of Pompeii, Italy, is the Pontifical Basilica to Our Lady of the Holy Rosary, and it is the only basilica in the world built by a former Satanist. Blessed Bartolo Longo spent years of his life restoring the original Church of Our Lady of the Holy Rosary, and then replacing it with a larger shrine, in thanksgiving for being saved from Satanism by Our Lady.

Bartolo Longo's life is testimony to the power of the Most Holy Rosary to heal very serious, very deep wounds inflicted by the devil and sin. Bartolo was born on 10th February 1841, the son of Italian parents, Dr Bartolomeo Longo and Antonina Luparelli, who were devout Catholics who prayed the Rosary together daily as a family.

Bartolo's father died when he was 10 years old. His mother remarried, and Bartolo began to drift away from the faith. During his studies at Naples University, Bartolo became involved with the occult, taking part in séances, fortune-telling and sexual promiscuity. Many of his lecturers were ex-priests who expressed intense hatred of the Church. Bartolo writes:

> I, too, grew to hate monks, priests and the Pope, and in particular I detested the Dominicans, the most formidable, furious opponents of those great modern professors, proclaimed by the university the sons of progress, the defenders of science, the champions of every sort of freedom. (Fr Roger J Landry, *From Satanist to Saint*)

He was drawn deeper into occult practices, becoming a member of a satanic cult, and eventually he was initiated into the satanic priesthood. For years he presided over satanic services, blasphemously condemning God and the Catholic Church as "evil". His hatred of the faith drove him to seek out and attempt to persuade Catholics to leave the Church. Bartolo Longo was an apostle of Satan.

However, like many involved in the occult and satanism, Bartolo was afflicted with demonic oppression, which was ruining his life. People suffering from demonic oppression experience self-destructive thoughts, self-harming, the urge to actions that are damaging to themselves and others. Bartolo has been described as suffering "despair, fear, hate, anger, an inability to forgive, resentment, and thoughts of suicide".

Power of a family's love, power of the Rosary

Bartolo Longo's family tried to persuade him to leave his self-destructive way of life, praying for him constantly. Sinking deeper into self-destructive darkness, one day Bartolo heard the voice of his dead father beseeching him, "Return to God! Return to God!"

Professor Vincenzo Pepe, a friend from his home town, put Bartolo in touch with a Dominican priest, Friar Alberto Radente, who taught him about the healing power of the Most Holy Rosary. Fr Radente said to him: "If you are looking for salvation, propagate the Rosary. It is the promise of Mary. He who propagates the Rosary shall be saved."

At the age of 30, on 7th October 1871, the feast of Our Lady of the Rosary, Bartolo became a Dominican tertiary and took the name "Rosario". Bartolo prayed to Our Lady, "I shall not depart from this earth without first displaying before you the triumph of your Rosary."

Following his return to the Catholic faith, Bartolo went one last time to a séance, at which he held up a rosary and declared, "I renounce spiritualism because it is nothing but a maze of error and falsehood." However, he still struggled with agonising guilt about his years as a satanist priest and his blasphemy against God. Of those times he wrote:

One day in the fields around Pompeii, I recalled my former condition as a priest of Satan... I thought that perhaps as the priesthood of Christ is for eternity, so also the priesthood of Satan is for eternity. So, despite my repentance, I thought: I am still consecrated to Satan, and I am still his slave and property as he awaits me in Hell. As I pondered over my condition, I experienced a deep sense of despair and almost committed suicide. Then I heard an echo in my ear of the voice of Friar Alberto repeating the words of the Blessed Virgin Mary: "One who propagates my Rosary shall be saved." Falling to my knees, I exclaimed: "If your words are true that he who propagates your Rosary will be saved, I shall reach salvation because I shall not leave this earth without propagating your Rosary."

From that day Bartolo dedicated his life to bringing the light of Christ, through the Most Holy Rosary, to those Catholics in the town of Pompeii trapped by the same superstition and dark practices. To this end, Bartolo promoted devotion to the Rosary by forming a Confraternity of the Rosary, by restoring a dilapidated church dedicated to Our Lady of the Rosary and by personally sponsoring an annual festival in honour of Our Lady of the Rosary. Of the saving power of the Rosary Bartolo wrote:

The Rosary could very well be called the poem of human redemption. The Rosary is a poem that takes its lively but simplistic hues from the pure palette of the Gospel...

Bartolo also established the Marian devotion of the 'Supplication to the Queen of Victories', first prayed in Pompeii in October 1883, and now recited all over the world on 8th May and on the first Sunday in October.

As well as these Spiritual Works of Mercy, Bartolo Longo was inspired by his deep love for Our Lady and the Church to radical Corporal Works of Mercy. In the words of Pope St John Paul II, Bartolo transformed Pompeii into "a living citadel of human and Christian goodness". He established a number of religious and charitable institutions, among them an orphanage, the Sons of Prisoners and the Daughters of Prisoners hospices, the Daughters of the Holy Rosary of Pompeii, and the Dominican Tertiaries.

In 1875 Bartolo received a special grace when Father Radente gave him a painting of Our Lady of the Rosary. The painting portrays Mary seated on a throne holding the child Jesus and handing a rosary to St Dominic and St Catherine of Siena, who are standing at her feet. The moment Bartolo hung the painting in the church, miracles began to happen. On the very first day, 12-year-old Clorinda Lucarelli was completely healed of epileptic seizures diagnosed as incurable. A year after that first miracle, Bartolo began the construction of a larger church that was completed in 1891, becoming the Pontifical Basilica of Our Lady of the Most Holy Rosary of Pompeii.

Bartolo "Rosario" Longo died in 1926 at the age of 85. His final words were, "My only desire is to see Mary who saved me and who will save me from the clutches of Satan."

When he was a priest of satan, Bartolo Longo was desperately sick, under the power of satan. His conversion and his amazing apostolate in Pompeii witness to the power of the Most Holy Rosary. When Catholics are really suffering, really going through dark times, many, if not most, turn to Our Lady and her Rosary. This is a common Catholic experience for three reasons – we know Mary is our mother; we also know that we can get closer to Jesus through his mother; and we know that the Most Holy Rosary is the best medicine for the times when we or our loved ones are sick, physically, morally and spiritually. My family prays the Rosary daily, including prayers for the conversion of members of our extended family who have left the Church.

Dorothy Day, Servant of God

Dorothy Day co-founded, with Peter Maurin, the Catholic Worker Movement, an association of communities of lay people who "live in accordance with the justice and charity of Jesus Christ". She also started *The Catholic Worker* newspaper and opened houses of hospitality for the poor across the USA. Her cause for sainthood was opened in 2000.

Dorothy Day was born in New York in 1897 to Grace Satterlee Day and John Day, a sports journalist. Though her family were not churchgoers, she grew up in a Protestant environment, with her father passionately anti-Catholic.

My heart leaped when I heard the name of God

In her autobiography, *The Long Loneliness*, Dorothy Day describes her life as "being haunted by God", even though her family were not practising Christians in the sense of being part of a Christian community:

How much did I hear of religion as a child? Very little, and yet my heart leaped when I heard the name of God. I do believe every soul has a tendency toward God. "As soon as a man recalls the Godhead, a certain sweet movement fills his heart. Our understanding has never such great joy as when thinking of God," as St Francis de Sales writes. (*The Long Loneliness*, p. 120)

At the age of 10 Dorothy started to attend the local Episcopal church, where she studied the catechism so she could be baptised and confirmed. She writes in another autobiographical work, *From Union Square to Rome*, that one of the most formative memories of her childhood was coming across a Catholic neighbour praying:

> Mrs Barrett gave me my first impulse toward Catholicism. It was around ten o'clock in the morning that I went up to Kathryn's to call for her to come out and play. There was no one on the porch or in the kitchen. The breakfast dishes had all been washed. They were long railroad apartments, those flats, and thinking the children must be in the front room, I burst in and ran through the bedrooms. In the front room, Mrs Barrett was on her knees, saying her prayers. She turned to tell me that Kathryn and the children had all gone to the store and went on with her praying. And I felt a warm burst of love toward Mrs Barrett that I have never forgotten, a feeling of gratitude and happiness that still warms my heart when I remember her. She had God, and there was beauty and joy in her life. All through my life what she was doing remained with me. (*From Union Square to Rome*, pp. 24-25)

Lost at university

At the age of 16, Dorothy won a scholarship and enrolled at the University of Illinois. While at university she embraced Communism and rejected organised religion as a prop for the weak and also because it didn't do enough to alleviate the suffering of the poor. She believed that all of man's sufferings could be solved by politics.

Dorothy dropped out of university, became a journalist and social activist – spending time in jail for protesting for women's rights – and led a sexually promiscuous bohemian lifestyle which she later described as "dissolute, wasted, full of sensation and sensuality". She had live-in relationships with a number of men, and had an illegal abortion at the age of 21, which she regretted all her life. In one letter she wrote, Dorothy admitted:

> Twice I tried to take my own life, and the dear Lord pulled me through that darkness – I was rescued from that darkness. My sickness was physical too, since I had had an abortion with bad after-effects, and in a way my sickness of mind was a penance I had to endure. (*All the Way to Heaven: The Selected Letters of Dorothy Day*)

Pursued by God

One of Dorothy's favourite drinking companions was the Irish playwright Eugene O'Neill, who one cold winter night in 1917 recited Francis Thompson's poem, *Hound of Heaven*. The poem opened Dorothy's eyes to the possibility that God was pursuing her:

> It is one of those poems that awakens the soul, recalls to it the fact that God is its destiny. The idea of this pursuit fascinated me; the inevitableness of it, the recurrence of it, made me feel that inevitably I would have to pause in the mad rush of living to remember my first beginning and last end. (*From Union Square to Rome*)

Even though she described herself as a Communist, Dorothy was increasingly drawn to religion, and especially the devotions of ordinary Catholics. The seed that was planted by observing the Catholic Mrs Barrett kneeling at her prayers began to put down deeper roots and raise a tentative shoot of faith:

> It is certain that I felt the need to go to church more often, to kneel, to bow my head in prayer. A blind instinct, one might say, because I was not conscious of praying. But I went, I slipped into the atmosphere of prayer.

In due course, Dorothy acquired the Most Holy Rosary in New Orleans, carried it in her pocket, and addressed the Blessed Virgin whose statue she had been given.

Turning point for Dorothy

Dorothy bought a beach house with the proceeds from selling the film rights to a book, and settled there with her lover, Foster Batterham, a strident atheist. Her religious awakening gradually unfolded in response to the beauty of nature, leading to a growing awareness of God.

Her gradual returning to faith intensified when she found herself pregnant with baby Tamar. She was determined that her baby daughter would have the protection and direction in life bestowed by the Catholic faith that her life had lacked until that moment:

> I did not want my child to flounder as I had often floundered. I wanted to believe, and I wanted my child to believe, and if belonging to a Church would give her so inestimable a grace as faith in God, and the companionable love of the Saints, then the thing to do was to have her baptised a Catholic.

Dorothy prayed the Rosary more devoutly, attended Mass and read the classic work on Catholic discipleship, Thomas à Kempis's *The Imitation of Christ*. And she prayed for the gift of faith, admitting, "I was sure, yet not sure. I postponed the day of decision."

As a militant atheist, Dorothy's lover, Foster Batterham, was totally opposed to religion, and became increasingly alienated by her pregnancy and her determination to raise their baby as a Catholic. The birth of Tamar was the pivotal moment in Dorothy's awakening to the Catholic faith. Her friendship with a nun, Sister Aloysia, was also a decisive influence in her conversion. Sister Aloysia served at a Catholic refuge for unwed mothers, and came down to Dorothy's beach house when Foster was away, to teach her the Catechism. Against Foster's strong objections, Dorothy presented baby Tamar for baptism. Though she loved Foster deeply, he was forcing her to choose between him and her love for the Catholic faith.

Foster deserted Dorothy and his baby a number of times in reaction to her embracing the Catholic faith, but always he returned to them. The stress of Foster's hostility made Dorothy ill. They eventually separated. Dorothy went to Sister Aloysia and was conditionally baptised, as she had already been baptised in the Episcopal Church. Returning to New York, Dorothy was confirmed and entered into the full communion of the Catholic Church. From that moment, Dorothy searched for ways of using her talents and faith to serve the poor.

One of Dorothy Day's favourite passages from St Augustine captures her sense of coming home to God: "You have made our hearts for yourself, O God, and they will never rest until they rest in you" (St Augustine, *Confessions*).

Famous Christians who got lost and came back: Prayer reflections

Blessed Charles de Foucauld, pray for me and my family.

Blessed Bartolo Longo, pray for me and my family.

Dorothy Day, Servant of God, pray for me and my family.

Facing problems caused when family leave the Church

There is no hiding from the fact that a family that practises the faith is deeply hurt when a member of that family leaves the Church and rejects the Catholic faith. The break with the family can be a gradual drifting apart or a dramatic shock. When the casual or definite decision to stop being Catholic comes out into the open, there can be angry scenes, heart-breaking grief or just quiet, resigned acceptance.

I've known parents so overwhelmed by a sense of failure when a child rejects the faith that they themselves stop going to Mass because they feel they've let God down. They feel that somehow they are to blame, that there was some failure in their child's upbringing for which they are responsible. But as we've seen in the lives of Charles de Foucauld and Bartolo Longo, the family is more often than not blameless. Both Foucauld and Longo came from devout Catholic families, and were immersed in the Catholic way of life, but quickly lost their way the moment they left their families to go to college or university. This remains the experience of many Catholic families, that children lose their faith when they go away to university.

The communion of the family is wounded, sometimes definitively broken when a family member leaves the Church. Those who remain faithful experience the pain of this broken communion when faced with the empty bench at Mass or when sitting round the family table where lapsed children and grandchildren sit in awkward, uneasy silence as the rest of the family shares the prayer of grace before the meal. At these moments there is no denying the distance that has grown between members of the family who still love each other very much. This awareness of the broken communion within the family becomes an even greater source of anguish with the realisation that it mirrors the children's and grandchildren's broken relationship with God. It is natural on these occasions to be left feeling helpless, fearing for their future.

Waking people up from the sleeping sickness of unbelief

The danger is that, for the sake of peace in the family, the remaining faithful members sink into a practical indifference. There is the temptation to ignore the

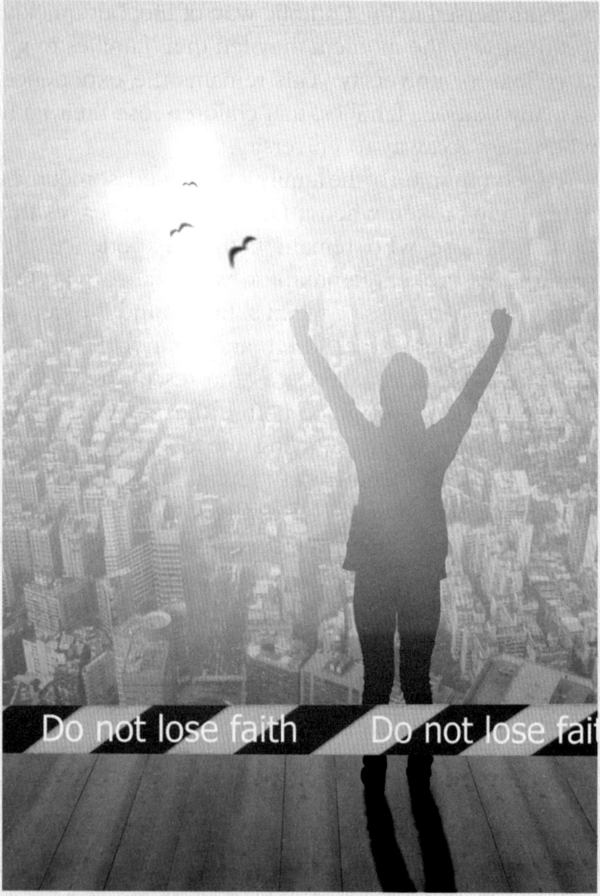

practical atheism of those who leave by focusing on their positive qualities and natural good acts, overlooking the fact that they are gravely lost, living their lives as if God does not exist. The danger for us is that if, out of love, and for the sake of peace, we acquiesce to their leaving the Church, we also live as if God does not exist.

Our silence, out of fear of causing upset or even a rift, can make us complicit in their damaging mistake. If we truly love them we have to face the truth that their lives are never made better by choosing to reject God in favour of unbelief.

Pope Benedict XVI gave a homily in 2005 about our responsibility to care about those who get lost, and the need to warn them of the danger in which they are placing themselves. The Holy Father went on to quote from St Augustine:

> I often have to pester you and to seem to be unpleasant, indeed, unkind toward you. And yet at the same time, he said, the image I have in my mind is of someone suffering from sleeping sickness. In that condition, a person is in danger of falling asleep for good, of falling into the sleep of death; he can only be saved by being constantly awakened. And he will say to whoever rouses him and wakes him up: leave me alone, I just want to sleep, leave me in peace. He will resist whoever is importunate

enough to wake him, when all he wants to do is sleep. (Quoted in D Vincent Twomey, SVD, *Pope Benedict XVI: The Conscience of Our Age*, p. 180)

Pope Benedict XVI drew the following conclusions from St Augustine's parable of waking someone with sleeping sickness:

Augustine's conclusion is that, if I really love the sick person, ...I cannot give in to his wishes; I cannot abandon him to what would be fatal for him. This seems to me to be a powerful metaphor for the sleep of unbelief, for our religious forgetfulness, indeed for our sleeping sickness with regard to the living God. Modern man does not want to be bothered with God. It is so comfortable – it seems – to live without God. And yet, if we let people fall into this sleeping sickness, then they will be lost and they will destroy not only themselves but also the possibility of creating any human community. For this reason, we cannot accept this religious forgetfulness; we must become disagreeable; we must over and over again, wrench people out of their religious forgetfulness. We have to wake them up and keep placing God – urgently and audibly – before their eyes and before their souls. (Quoted in D Vincent Twomey, SVD, *Pope Benedict XVI: The Conscience of Our Age*, pp. 180-181)

Having said this, every parent knows that when attempting to wake someone up, you have to tailor your approach to the personality and temperament of the person. Some just need a gentle call to wake them up, and a cup of tea placed by the bed; while others need, and will accept as reasonable, a loud voice and determined shaking. Sometimes we have even to become disagreeable when someone refuses to move, by pulling the duvet off them.

Whatever we do to wake our loved ones up from the sleeping sickness of unbelief we must do with love and genuine care towards them, judging what is appropriate and sensible in each situation.

Life is a serious business

It is essential that we keep in mind that life for each one of us is a serious business, a matter of attaining a joyful life in heaven or an eternal death in hell. It is understandable that some people panic when facing this supernatural reality of our lives in the context of loved ones who have left the Church. Two responses are not helpful – to deny that hell exists and assume that everyone goes to heaven or to judge that everyone who leaves the Church will definitely go to hell. Neither of these responses is true.

We cannot ignore that hell exists

There should be no doubt about the fact that hell exists. Both the Old Testament and the New Testament are explicitly clear that hell and eternal punishment for sin exist. Jesus himself speaks of "the unquenchable fire" reserved for those who refuse to believe and be converted (*Mt* 5:22, 29; 10:28; 13:42, 50; *Mk* 9:43-48). Furthermore, Jesus warns that he will pronounce condemnation on those who do not live and love as he lives and loves: "Depart from me, you cursed, into the eternal fire!" (*Mt* 25:41)

The idea of eternal punishment for sins often raises the objection that surely this is unjust and not the action of a loving God? However, the existence of hell is based on one fundamental truth – God's unconditional respect for the freedom of his creature, man. Ultimately, each one of us is responsible for our own destiny. As Pope Benedict expresses it, "Heaven reposes upon freedom and so leaves to the damned the right to will their own damnation" (Joseph Ratzinger, *Eschatology: Death and Eternal Life*, p. 216).

The other thing to keep in mind is that God has done everything possible to assist us to freely choose a life that will lead to heaven, even to the point of becoming man and dying on the cross to save us from the consequences of our own sins.

Pope Benedict XVI writes that it is important that we all "recognise the possibility of hell, of the radical and definitive failure of life" because it makes us recognise "the possibility and necessity for purification" through repentance for sin (Meeting with the parish priests and the clergy of the Diocese of Rome, February 2008).

We cannot deny that God wants to save everyone

The actions of God show us, and Sacred Scripture and Tradition testify, that God wants to save everyone: "In this is love, not that we loved God but that he loved us and sent his Son to be the expiation for our sins" (*1 Jn* 4:10). And the Church affirms, "There is not, never has been, and never will be a single human being for whom Christ did not suffer" (*CCC*, 605).

As we have seen earlier, God comes in search of the lost, who are the focus of his special, loving attention. At any moment, up to the moment of death, anyone who has rejected God, anyone who has left the Church, can avail themselves of the salvation won for each one of us through Christ's death on the cross. God longs for the salvation of every soul that he has so lovingly created, for whom he has sacrificed his Son, to whom he eagerly offers the life and joy of the Holy Spirit.

The *Catechism of the Catholic Church*, in a number of places, encourages us to hope in God's will to save everyone if they repent of their sin:

By ways known to him alone, God can provide the opportunity for salutary repentance. (*CCC*, 2283)

The Church implores the mercy of God, who does not want "any to perish, but all to come to repentance". (*2 P* 3:9; *CCC*, 1037)

The gospel account of the penitent thief and the impenitent thief crucified with Our Lord sets out the choice facing all of us before the moment of death (*Lk* 23:39-43). The impenitent thief hardens his heart, despairs and blasphemes, while the penitent thief repents of his life of sin, acknowledges the reality of God, prays to Jesus for help, and is immediately and readily promised salvation.

Those that harden their hearts

The most challenging problem for families is how to respond to those who are hostile towards the Church and argumentative about the faith. The secularism and scientism of the prevailing culture encourages an aggressive attitude towards the Catholic faith. This can be a cause of endless arguments, point-scoring and upsetting mockery. It can get to the point that just being with members of the family who remain practising Catholics can trigger a tense atmosphere of passive aggression.

It's as if being anti-Catholic becomes the new "faith" for some that leave the Church. St John Chrysostom wrote, "For he who says goodbye to the Christian life, devises for himself a faith which accords with his moral conduct" (*Homily on 1 Tm*). And G K Chesterton observed, "When men choose not to believe in God, they do not thereafter believe in nothing, they then become capable of believing in anything."

Sometimes Catholics who have left the Church get caught up in increasingly popular paganism, Wicca and satanism, which, while inherently hostile to Christianity and the Catholic Church, cater to their need for ritual and "spirituality". But as the testimony of Blessed Bartolo Longo shows, even those lost in such lifestyles can be reached through persistent love, consistent prayer and the right intervention at the right time.

The real problem is that by accepting the culture's general ill-feeling and hostility towards the faith, those who leave the Church harden their hearts against God. Sacred Scripture warns of the danger of hardened hearts:

O that today you would listen to his voice, harden not your hearts. (*Ps* 95:7-8)

Be careful then, dear brothers and sisters. Make sure that your own hearts are not evil and unbelieving, turning you away from the living God. But exhort one another every day, as long as it is called "today", that none of you may be hardened by the deceitfulness of sin. (*Heb* 3:12-13)

Hardness of heart is not restricted to Catholics who leave the Church, but is also a danger to those who remain members, but whose hearts are closed to love (see *Lumen Gentium*, 14). Our Lord is angered and grieved when he finds hardened hearts among those who should know better:

And he looked around at them with anger, grieved at their hardness of heart. (*Mk* 3:5)

Those who choose to close their hearts to God, often through pride and thinking they know better than his self-revelation, put themselves in a bad way because they deliberately resist God's grace. By doing so, they block repentance and conversion, putting themselves in danger of mortal sin, and hell.

Mortal sin requires *full knowledge* and *complete consent*. It presupposes knowledge of the sinful character of the act, of its opposition to God's law. It also implies a consent sufficiently deliberate to be a personal choice. Feigned ignorance and hardness of heart (*Mk* 3:5-6; *Lk* 16:19-31) do not diminish, but rather increase, the voluntary character of a sin. (*CCC*, 1859)

Please do not despair or panic when you read about the seriousness of a heart hardened against God. No one is beyond the love and forgiveness of God, who constantly seeks in so many ways to break through the hardest bitterness against him.

What can a family do when loved ones put themselves in this desperate situation? I take hope in the gospel account of Our Lord's cure of the paralysed man, because Jesus was moved by the faith of his friends:

And behold, men were bringing on a bed a man who was paralysed, and they sought to bring him in and lay him before Jesus; but finding no way to bring him in, because of the crowd, they went up on the roof and let him down with his bed through the tiles into the midst before Jesus. And when he saw their faith he said, "Man, your sins are forgiven you." (*Lk* 5:18-20)

God looks for faith in order to act in a situation, because he respects the freedom of choice he has given his creatures. Even if our loved ones have blocked God's grace to act by their hardness of heart, our intercessory prayers, our personal sacrifices out of love for them, make space for God's grace to work. St Ambrose puts it like this:

> How great is the Lord who on account of the merits of some pardons others, and while praising the former, absolves the latter. (St Ambrose, *Expositio Evangelii sec. Lucam*)

Through our faith, our prayers and our sacrifices for our loved ones who have left the Church, God can work miracles.

Facing problems caused when family leave the Church: Prayer reflections

Lord, show me your will so in love and care I may wake those who are sleeping, dead to your word.

Lord, help my heart to be good and believing.

May my faith help those around me.

Jesus, I trust in you.

Jesus, I surrender myself to you.

Let your will be done.

Jesus, take care of everything.

Tips about coping
when family leave

Love them for their own sake

I've seen adult children of faithful Catholic parents exasperated and further alienated from Our Lord and the Catholic faith because mum or dad have been overbearing about coming back to the Church. It is understandable that parents are upset and anxious about their children losing the faith, but if this drives you to pressure your children about the faith every time you see them it will do more harm than good. Love them for their own sake: "If they feel our love, they will believe what we say" (Bl. Rupert Mayer). Frequently meditate on St Paul's great hymn to Christian love (*1 Co* 13).

When children become enemies of the faith

Some parents have to cope with children who are zealous proponents of atheism and scientism, sometimes known as the New Atheism, or advocates of New Age beliefs, such as Wicca. It is not uncommon for those who have ideologically hardened their hearts to take every opportunity to attack and mock Catholic beliefs. They even try to convert family members who remain Catholic to their new "faith". In this sense, they become enemies of the faith. This is a hard truth to admit, but it is necessary if you are to remain strong in the faith during the battering, subtle or crude, that you may receive at the hands of children or other family members who have become enemies of what we hold to be most precious.

The danger in this situation is that the family could be broken by the conflict that is brought into the family home. There are two actions to take in this situation. Firstly, remember that Our Lord showed a special love for his enemies, and that he made it a condition of our discipleship that we also have a special love for enemies (*Lk* 6:27-36). However, this does not mean that you put yourself in the way of harm, and sometimes you may need to love from a distance.

Secondly, consecrate, or re-consecrate, your family, especially those who are lost or who have become enemies of the faith, to the Sacred Heart of Our Lord Jesus Christ (*https://www.ewtn.com/faith/teachings/incab3b.htm*). Enthrone the Sacred Heart of Jesus in your home through a blessed sacred image or a statue.

Our Lord promised St Margaret Mary Alacoque, "I will bless every place where an image of my Sacred Heart will be exposed and honoured." The Sacred Heart of Jesus at the centre of the family home is a powerful antidote to the ingratitude, contempt, irreverence, sacrileges and coldness of those who harden their hearts against Our Lord and his Church.

Ask Our Lord for help

Vernon Robertson, host of EWTN's "How to Pray for your Sons and Daughters and Loved Ones", proposes a simple but powerful suggestion to parents and grandparents coping with loved ones who leave the Church. Vernon looks to Our Lord's encounter with the Canaanite woman (*Mt* 15:21-28). This mother asked Jesus to heal her daughter who was "severely possessed by a demon". Possession by a demon is the most extreme form of alienation from God. The mother's persistence in asking for help, and her faith in the power of Our Lord to save her daughter, elicits this response from Jesus, "O woman, great is your faith! Be it done for you as you desire", and the immediate healing of the daughter (*Mt* 15:28).

St Josemaría Escrivá advises, "Persevere in prayer. Persevere, even when your efforts seem barren. Prayer is always fruitful" (*The Way*, 101). Vernon Robertson advises us not to get discouraged if our prayers don't bear fruit immediately, recommending that we view them from the perspective of God's time and purpose.

Benefit from this great age of divine mercy

We are blessed to be living during a great age of divine mercy, inaugurated by apparitions and messages of Our Lady and the visions of Our Lord and his messages concerning his divine mercy to St Faustina Kowalska (1905-1938). Also, Pope St John Paul II established Divine Mercy Sunday so that the Church could celebrate this great age of divine mercy towards sinful mankind.

Confirming that Our Lord has a special love for the lost, Jesus revealed to St Faustina that he would rather be merciful than just towards repentant sinners. St Faustina gave this message from Our Lord, exhorting us to pray this prayer for mercy at 3 p.m. each day in honour of his death on the cross:

> If you say this prayer, with a contrite heart and with faith, on behalf of some sinner, I will give that soul the grace of conversion, "O blood and water that gushed forth from the heart of Jesus, as a fount of mercy for us, I trust in You."

Heaven's concern for the salvation of sinners was also expressed in Our Lady of Fatima's messages to the three little children. Our Lady asks us to make reparation for our own sins and for sinners. Acts of reparation are prayers and sacrifices to repair or make up for sinful offences against God. Our Lady gave five prayers of reparation which enable us to make up for our own sins and the sins of others who have rejected God. Here are two of them, which can be said for loved ones who have left the Church:

> O my Jesus, forgive us our sins, save us from the fires of hell, lead all souls to heaven, especially those in the most need of Thy mercy.

> My God, I believe, I adore, I trust and I love Thee! I beg pardon for all those that do not believe, do not adore, do not trust and do not love Thee.

Pray an intercessory Rosary

There is a long tradition of praying to Mary to ask for her maternal intercession, her motherly prayers for our needs, particularly our heartfelt needs, such as the conversion of children and family members who have left the faith. This practice can be traced back to Our Lady interceding for the newly married couple at Cana, an event that "clearly shows the power of Mary's intercession as she makes known to Jesus the needs of others: 'They have no wine' (*Jn* 2:3)" (Pope St John Paul II, *Rosarium Virginis Mariae*, 16). Mary is alert to the needs of others, especially the cries of mothers and fathers for their children:

> The Rosary is both meditation and supplication. Insistent prayer to the Mother of God is based on confidence that her maternal intercession can obtain all things from the heart of her Son. When in the Rosary we plead with Mary, the sanctuary of the Holy Spirit (cf. *Lk* 1:35), she intercedes for us before the Father who filled her with grace and before the Son born of her womb, praying with us and for us. (Pope St John Paul II, *Rosarium Virginis Mariae*, 16)

There are different ways of praying the Rosary as a way of interceding for loved ones who have left the Church. Some name those who are lost as part of the "Hail Mary": "Holy Mary, Mother of God, pray for us sinners, [name of loved one], now and at the hour of our death. Amen." Or you can name your family member before praying each "Hail Mary". Between us, my wife and I have almost a whole Rosary, fifty names of members of our joint extended families who have left the Church.

Be good shepherds and go in search of the lost

The truth at the heart of this booklet is that God comes looking for us when we get lost, when we rebel against him, and separate ourselves from his life and his love.

The Parable of the Good Shepherd and the Lost Sheep contains this fundamental truth about God's dealings with sinful, lost humanity.

Sacred Scripture shows us that God approaches sinful humanity in a certain, careful way, so as not to overwhelm us, and scare us away. We should study how God goes in search of humanity, so that we do likewise when members of our family get lost.

God is love, and expresses his love in the best way possible to create a relationship with man. God's revelation is not an ideology but an invitation to share his life. Likewise we should be sensitive to the personalities, temperaments and stages of life of loved ones who have left the Church. We're not asking them to sign up to an ideology, but to re-enter into a living relationship with God.

Tips about coping when family leave:
Prayer reflections

Lord, may I be filled with your pure love and meditate frequently on St Paul's great hymn to Christian love.

I consecrate my family, especially those who are lost or who have become enemies of the faith, to your Sacred Heart, my Lord Jesus Christ.

Lord, do not let me become discouraged, but let me persevere in prayer.

O blood and water that gushed forth from the heart of Jesus, as a fount of mercy for us, I trust in You.

O my Jesus, forgive us our sins, save us from the fires of hell, lead all souls to heaven, especially those in the most need of Thy mercy.

My God, I believe, I adore, I trust and I love Thee! I beg pardon for all those that do not believe, do not adore, do not trust and do not love Thee.

Holy Mary intercede on behalf of my family that we may be in a living relationship with the Most Holy Trinity.